Math - 8th

D0880265

Coin Games and Puzzles

by
Maxey Brooke

Dover Publications, Inc.
New York

Published in Canada by General Publishing Com-
pany, Ltd., 30 Lesmill Road, Don Mills, Toronto,
Ontario.
Published in the United Kingdom by Constable
and Company, Ltd., 10 Orange Street, London
WC 2.

This Dover edition, first published in 1973, is an
unabridged republication of the work originally
published by Charles Scribner's Sons in 1963 under
the title *Fun for the Money*.

International Standard Book Number: 0-486-22893-2

Manufactured in the United States of America
Dover Publications, Inc.
180 Varick Street
New York, N. Y. 10014

This one is for
Linda and Jamie

ACKNOWLEDGMENTS

Harper & Row: Mulac–The Game Book   2, 37
Association Press: Recreational Activities   3, 39, 40, 41
McGraw Hill (Whittlesey House): Leopold–At East   4
Dover Publications: Dudeney–Canterbury Puzzles   26
————–Amusements in Mathematics   34, 35, 36
Simon & Schuster: Kasner & Newman–Mathematics and the
    Imagination   10
World Book Company: Meyer–Fun With Mathematics   31
Emerson Books: Fegrazia–Math Is Fun   12
Houston Post: 1, 15
Scripta Mathematica: 43
Mathematical Gazette: 44
Dudeney, H. E.: 7, 8, 53–56

CONTENTS

Had I been born seventy-five years earlier, I would probably have been a Mississippi river boat gambler. Twenty-five years later, I might have been a computerman. But born when I was, I chose the most exciting profession available; engineering. An engineer spends his life solving, or trying to solve problems.

Whether being interested in puzzles made me an engineer or whether being an engineer made me a puzzle-smith, I'll never know. I like all kinds of puzzles; arithmetical puzzles, geometric puzzles, chess puzzles, alphametics, magic squares, and all the others.

But best of all, I like to draw a diagram, place some coins on it and challenge someone to solve the puzzle I propose.

For example, I call this one. . . . . .

TRIANGULAR JUMP

This problem is first for the pragmatic reason that it is the one that started this collection. I got it from George Fuerman's fabulous column "Post Card" in the Houston Post.

Place 14 coins on the diagram, leaving one blank space. Jump as in checkers in such a way as to leave only one coin when you finish. Dr. Wesley Edwards of the University of Houston says there are six possible solutions.

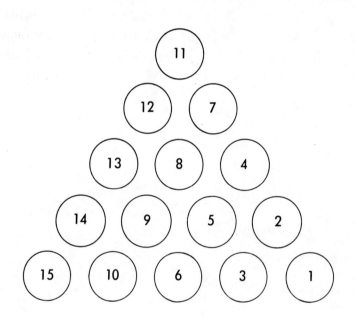

TRIANGULAR JUMP, LTD.

To continue with the triangle motif and to complicate matters, let us confine the moves to the diagonals and across the bottom. For example, a jump from 4 to 13 would be illegal. Otherwise the same rules apply.

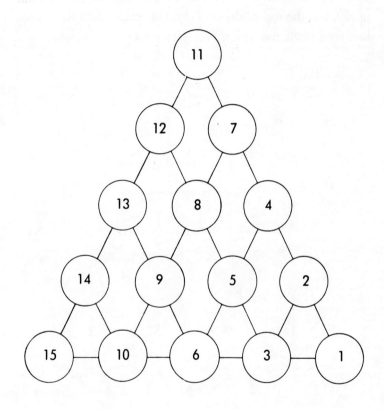

HEADLESS TRIANGLE

One thing always leads to another. Find a good coin game and someone comes along with complications. The TRIANGULAR JUMP is no exception. The same rules apply, but the top position (11) must be left vacant, and the last coin must end up on that very spot.

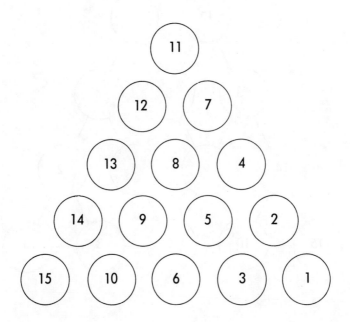

This is known as a "coffee winner". Bet someone a cup of coffee that he can't solve it. You'll win more than you'll lose. Form a triangle with ten pennies as shown. Reverse the triangle so that it points down instead of up, by moving only three pennies. Good hunting!

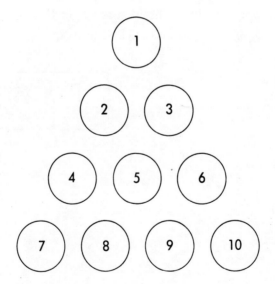

OLD TIMER

This is the first coin game I ever saw. My father showed it to me thirty-five years ago. Since then I have found it as a chess puzzle in a book dated 1882. Put three

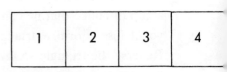

pennies in squares 1, 2, and 3. Put three nickels in squares 5, 6, and 7. Leave square 4 blank. The pennies can be moved only to the right and the nickels only to the left. A coin can move into an adjacent square or can jump over one of the opposite kind. The idea is to get the pennies into squares 5, 6, and 7 and the nickels into squares 1, 2, and 3.

5	6	7

Now try it with 9 squares with pennies in squares 1, 2, 3, and 4 and nickels in squares 6, 7, 8, and 9.

If you are interested in the mathematics of the thing, for n pennies and n nickels, $n(n+2)$ moves are needed.

5	6	7	8	9

THE FIEND

Like the Triangular Jump, people just couldn't leave well enough alone. Sam Loyd worked the OLD TIMER into what he called the Fore and Aft Game. The result is one of the most fiendishly complicated coin games ever invented. The pennies can be moved only to the right and down. The nickels only to the left and up. A coin can be moved to an adjacent empty square or can jump over one of the other kind. No diagonal moves are allowed. Now, interchange the coins.

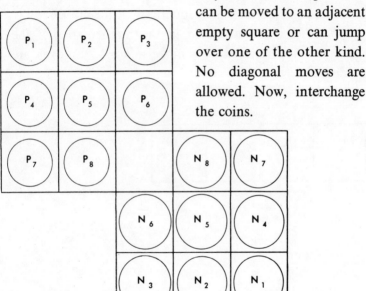

At every social gathering, from a formal dinner to a bunch of the guys having coffee at the local hash house, there comes a time when conversation lags. He who can cause the party to perk up at such times is much sought after.

When the dead spot appears, you can liven things up by taking four coins out of your pocket, arranging them in formation I and challenging anybody to move them to formation II. Each move consists of sliding a coin, without disturbing another, to a new position. The coins must remain flat and the formation must be exact, that is, as though there were a fifth coin in the position shown by the dotted circle. Moving the left bottom coin to the right is not the right move since it would be debatable that the new position in II was exact. Two moves are enough.

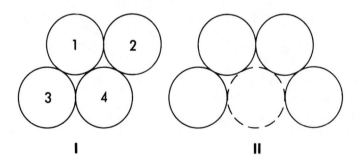

I　　　　　　　　　　　　II

19

Unfortunately, a trick will work only one time for each crowd. So if you want to keep up your reputation as a party pepper-upper, you need more than one trick. Here's another using five coins. Move them from formation I to formation II using the same rules as before.

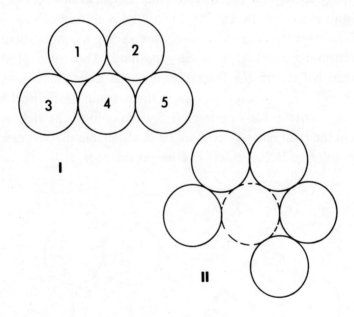

I

II

Now that your reputation is established, you must maintain it, and each trick must be trickier than the one before. So this time start with six coins. And only you need know the truth, this is the easiest of the three shifts.

Mr. Kobon Fijimuri of Osaka, Japan, tells me that SHIFTY and SHIFTIEST were invented by H. E. Dudeney in *Modern Puzzles and How to Solve Them,* while SHIFTIER is his own.

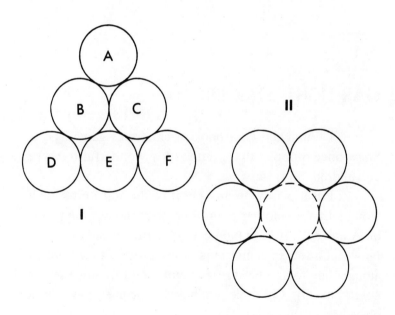

KAYLES • *10* •

This game was invented by the old master, H. E. Dudeney, who gave it a very fanciful history. But that is another story.

Our story goes like this: place 11 coins in a row, touching. The twelfth is set apart by the width of a coin. Players alternately draw one or two touching coins. The one who draws the last coin wins.

STAR LIGHT–STAR BRIGHT • *11* •

I found this in a book of children's games. G. B. Shaw once quipped that youth is too wonderful to waste on children. So is this trick.

Put a penny on any point of the star and slide it along a line to another point. For example, put the penny on A and slide it to D (you could alternately slide it to F). Now put another penny on any vacant point and slide it along a line to another vacant point (you can now use any point but D). Continue until seven pennies have been placed on seven points.

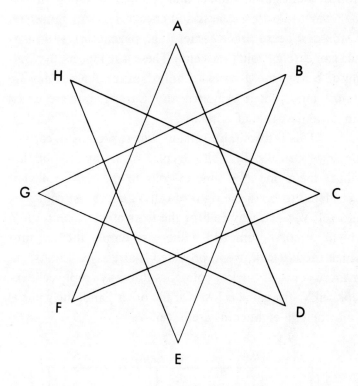

H. J. R. Murray in "A History of Board Games Other Than Chess" has classified all games into five basic groups: games of alignment and configuration (e.g. tic-tac-toe), war games (e.g., chess and checkers), hunt games, (e. g., fox and geese), race games (e.g., parcheesi), and mancula games (e.g. Gold Coast etc.). These last concern the dealing of beans into a series of holes and pockets. They are almost unknown in America and Europe, but are called the national game of Africa.

    This is a solitaire version. Put two coins in each of the first four cells. Take all the coins from any cell and distribute them one at a time in cells to the right. Cell I is considered to be to the right of cell V. If the last coin goes into cell V, select any cell for the next move except cell V which cannot be emptied. Otherwise empty the cell into which the last coin went, provided it already contains one or more coins. If the last coin goes into any empty cell, except cell V, the game is lost. On the other hand, the game is won when all eight coins are in cell V.

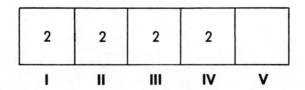

SIMPLE SIMON

This probably should not be in the collection. However, because it is so simple, it sometimes baffles people. Try it yourself, then try it on your friends.

Lay six coins in a row, the three on the left with heads up and the three on the right with tails up. The puzzle is to get them arranged with heads and tails alternating in three moves. Each move consists of turning over a pair of adjacent coins.

FROM JAPAN

I do not doubt the Japanese origin of this game, but the earliest reference is British in 1884. In any event it is pretty old.

Put four nickels and four pennies alternately in a line, almost touching. Move two adjacent coins together without altering their relative position. In four moves end up with a line of four pennies followed by four nickels.

Try it again, this time reversing the relative positions of the coins after each move. In five moves, end up with a line of four nickels followed by four pennies.

STACK'EM UP · *15* ·

This one is both a coffee winner and a party-pepper. If I were asked to name my favorite coin game, this would probably be it.

Place ten coins in a row. Jump any coin over the two next to it and on to the coin beyond. When you finish, you should have five stacks of two coins each spaced at equal distances.

If you want to count two coins in a stack as one, you can still solve the problem.

QUEEN'S X · *16* ·

If you're tired of moving coins around, try this static game. There are four coins in thirty-six squares so that no two coins are in a row—horizontal, vertical, or diagonal. How many other arrangements are possible, not counting mirror images or reversals?

Chess players will recognize this as a variation of the "eight queens problem" which requires placing 8 queens on a chessboard so that they cannot attack each other. The "eight queens" was first proposed by Max Bezzel. Gauss published such a masterful analysis of the problem that he generally gets credit for having originated it.

Unfortunately, I don't know who first proposed this problem and I doubt if it has been analyzed.

	a	b	c	d	e	f
1	◯					
2						
3						◯
4			◯			
5						
6				◯		

LINE'EM UP

This type of problem has been kicking around for more than two hundred years if we can believe the story that Sir Isaac Newton invented it. In its original form, it concerned how to plant a number of trees in the maximum number of rows of so many trees per row. Mathematicians call it "the n-in-a-row problem" and have yet to solve it.

With but a modicum of cunning, it can be made into coin problems, such as:

17. Arrange 9 coins in 10 rows of 3 each.
18. Arrange 10 coins in 5 rows of 4 each.
19. Arrange 12 coins in 7 rows of 4 each.
20. Arrange 16 coins in 15 rows of 4 each.
21. Arrange 18 coins in 9 rows of 5 each.
22. Arrange 11 coins in 16 rows of 3 each.
23. Arrange 21 coins in 12 rows of 5 each.
24. Arrange 22 coins in 21 rows of 4 each.

QUEEN'S X DOUBLED

On our Queen's X 6x6 grid, arrange the greatest number of coins possible so that:

1. There is only one coin in each square.
2. There are not more than two coins in any horizontal, vertical, or diagonal.

A recipe for cooking rabbits starts "first catch a rabbit."

First draw a square, a 5x5 square. Next add 9 coins. The trick is to remove 8 coins and leave a ninth coin in the center square. The removals are made by jumping one coin over another to a vacant square and removing the coin jumped. You can jump horizontally, vertically, or diagonally.

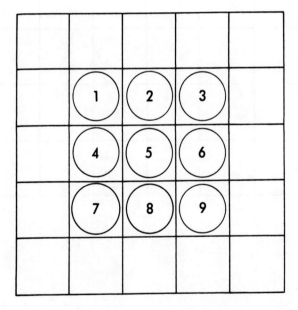

STILL STRICTLY FOR SQUARES

This time use a 4x4 square and add ten coins. Again remove all but one by jumping and removing the jumped coin. Diagonal jumps are not allowed. As the coins stand, you obviously cannot make a move. But you are permitted to transfer any single coin you wish to any vacant square before starting. Good luck!

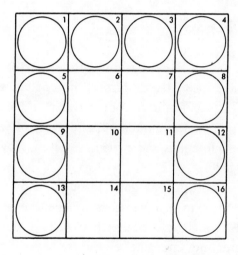

STACK'EM DEEP   • *28* •

Place twelve nickels in a row. The job is to stack them three deep without any move passing over more or less than fifteen cents.

Now try it with sixteen nickels. Stack them four deep by making twenty-cent jumps.

GOOD OLD JOE   • *29* •

We have a story that during the sack of Jotapata by Vespasian, Josephus hid himself in a cellar with forty other Jews. It was found that only two could survive. So they stood in a circle, counted off, and every fifteenth man killed himself. Josephus and a friend survived. How was the circle arranged?

This problem has gone through many variations and here it turns up as a coin game. Place four nickels and four pennies in a circle. Arrange them so that, starting with the top one and counting clockwise, every fifth coin removed will be a penny. If you remove every ninth coin, only nickels will be taken.

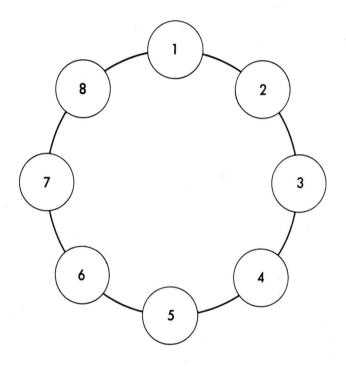

Place two dimes on squares 1 and 3; two pennies on squares 6 and 8. Move one coin at a time, in any order, along the lines from square to square until you have exchanged places. The dimes end up on squares 7 and 8 and the pennies on squares 1 and 3. Of course, no two coins can be on any one square at the same time.

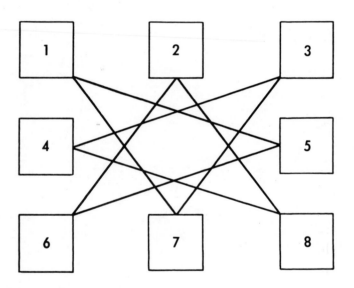

• 31 •   TAKE A RUNNING JUMP

Place three dimes in squares 2, 3, and 4; three
pennies in squares 5, 6, and 7. You can move to an unoccupied square, or jump over one or two coins to an unoccupied square. You can jump in either direction and a coin
can jump over its own value, the opposite value, or both
values. The object is to swap positions. Par for the course
is 10 jumps.

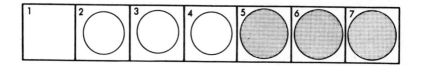

• 32 •   ROLL ME OVER

This is less of a game and more of a paradox. Use
it when you need a joke. If coin A is rolled around coin B,
will the "A" be upside down, upright, or sidewise when it
reaches the other side?

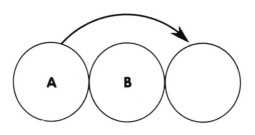

Place a coin on each intersection except 8. Jump as in checkers along any line and remove the coin jumped. End up with only one coin.

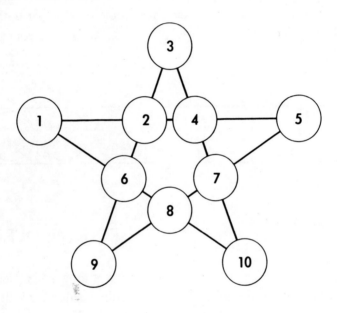

There is a pretty (but fictitious) legend about 64 plates of gold on three diamond needles below a temple in Benares. When they are moved from one needle to the next according to certain rules, the world will come to an end. But the number of moves is so preposterously large that the plates will probably wear out before the game is completed.

Here is a simplified version using coins. Make a pyramid of a half dollar (5), a quarter (4), a nickel (3), a penny (2), and a dime (1). The trick is to make a pyramid in another square, moving one coin at a time, and never putting a coin on one of a smaller size.

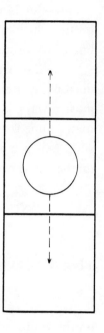

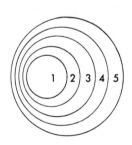

A LITTLE LIKE CHECKERS

Put 14 coins around the border of a checkerboard on the white squares; put 10 coins inside them on the next line of white squares.

Start with any man jumping forward or backward diagonally. Remove the man jumped. The jumping man must always land on the square immediately beyond the man jumped. However, any number of squares can intervene between the start of the jump and the man to be jumped. The object is to end up with only one man.

THE FIFTEENTH MAN

Put 14 coins around the border of a checkerboard on the white squares. Place a 15th man on any unoccupied square and jump as in Problem 35. Continue until only one man remains.

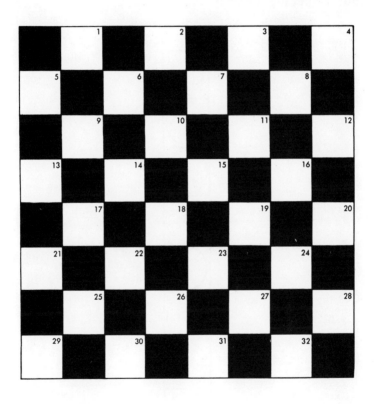

Eight numbered coins are on nine positions. The object is to shift the coins, either by single moves or jumps until the number order is reversed.

One player takes the pennies, the other takes the dimes. Move one square at a time. Play alternately, backward, forward, sideways, diagonally. You cannot jump. The one who gets five in a row horizontally, vertically, or diagonally, wins.

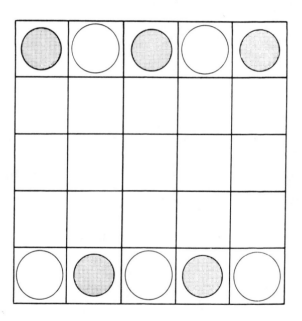

Place two dimes on points 1 and 2; two pennies on points 9 and 10. The game is to make the dimes and pennies change places. You can move the coins one at a time in any order you like, along the lines from point to point. The only restriction is that a dime and a penny may never stand on the same straight line. The opening move is from 1 or 2 to 3, or from 9 or 10 to 7. Take it from there in seventeen more moves.

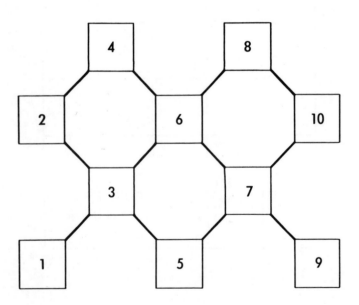

Most of the items in this collection are from books and articles on puzzles. Some come from bona fide mathematical magazines, this one is from *Scripta Mathematica.* I must admit that in its heyday, S.M. could be as pixyish as they come.

Shift the coins from H to O in the fewest number of moves. A move consists of sliding, without lifting, one and only one coin at a time, and without disturbing any of the other seven, leave it touching two others. This can be done in five moves.

The second problem is to get back from O to H in the same manner. Oddly enough, seven moves are required.

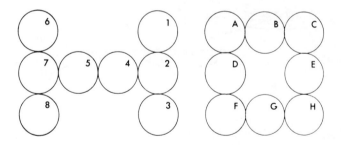

THE FALSE COIN

We have eleven good coins and one counterfeit. It matches the others in everything but weight. There is a scheme by which we can determine the counterfeit coin in only three weighings and tell whether it is heavy or light. The weighings are shown below. Which is the counterfeit coin, and is it heavier or lighter than the others?

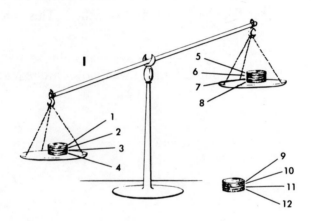

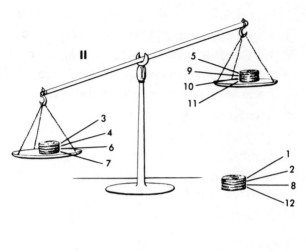

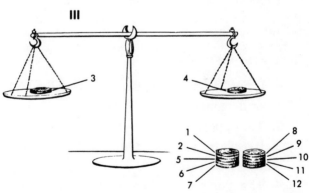

I have tried to classify games according to mode of capture. To date I have ten methods:

1. Displacement as in Chess
2. En Passant—special move in Chess
3. Short leap as in Checkers
4. Long leap as in Polish Checkers
5. The Kono jump
6. Interception as in Mill
7. Sandwich as in Reversi
8. Intersection as in Baroque
9. Scissors as in Hasami Shogi
10. Withdrawal as in Fanorona

I use the last as a basis of this game. On a checker-board place 8 dimes and 8 pennies as shown in the diagram.

Play by these rules:

1. Coins move one square horizontally, vertically, or diagonally.
2. The opposing coin moved away from is captured.
3. If a player cannot capture an opposing coin he forfeits his turn.
4. The game ends when neither player can move without making a capture.
5. The winner is the one with the most pieces remaining on the board.

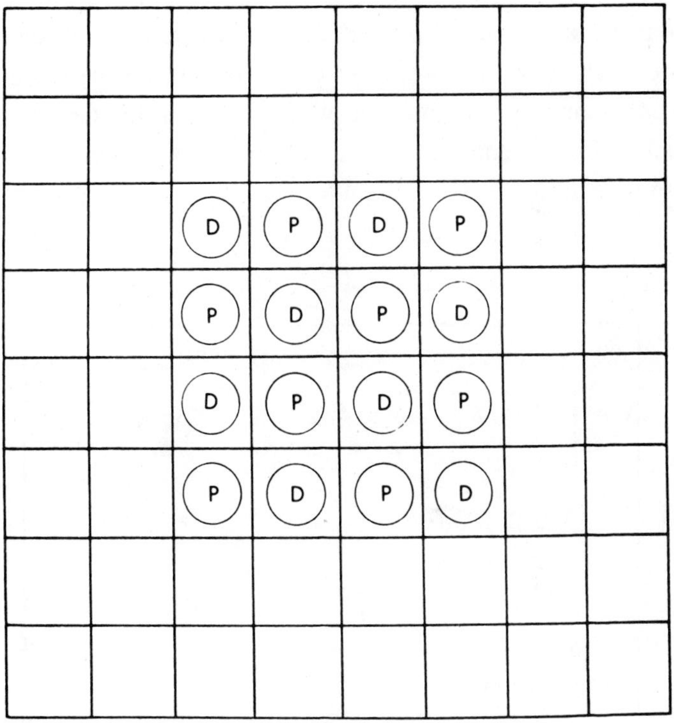
D P D P
P D P D
D P D P
P D P D

This British problem, originated by W. T. Whyte, concerns halfpennies. However, in this country quarters can be used. On a 5x3 inch file card or a 5x3 rectangle drawn on a sheet of paper, lay a quarter. Now a quarter is exactly one inch in diameter, so one inch from the first quarter, lay a second quarter. The third quarter is exactly one inch from the second, etc. No quarter can touch another or cross the boundary. The illustration shows one such arrangement, but not the best. How many quarters can you put on a 3x5 rectangle?

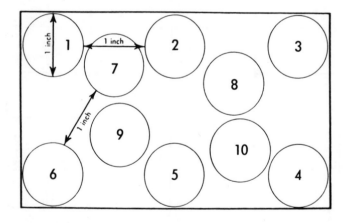

• 44 •   MAGIC SQUARE

This is a magic square. The rows, columns, and diagonals all total 65. For our trick, arrange five pennies, five nickels, five dimes, five quarters, and five half dollars so that each row, column, and diagonal will total ninety-one cents.

When you finish this, try putting two coins in each square so the total of each row, column, and diagonal will be $1.82.

17	24	1	8	15
23	5	7	14	16
4	6	13	20	22
10	12	19	21	3
11	18	25	2	9

• 45 •   ONE, TWO, THREE

This game used to be popular in Kansas City. It may still be. Any number can play. Each player has three coins. At a given signal, each extends his fist in which he has 0, 1, 2, or 3 coins. Each man guesses the total number of coins held. If a man guesses the correct total, he is eliminated. This continues until everybody but one is eliminated. The last man buys the coffee.

STUPIDITY • *46* •

Here's a silly little game I invented one rainy afternoon. Put three coins in cells 1 and 4, two coins in cells 2 and 5, and one coin in cells 3 and 6. Take the coins out of cell 1 and distribute them one by one in the cells, going clockwise (2, 3, 4). Take the coins out of the cell just beyond the one you put the last coin in (5) and distribute them clockwise. Continue until you get back to the original configuration.

It doesn't prove anything, but it will pass the time.

1	2	3
4	5	6

CHANGE • *47* •

How many ways can you make change for a dollar, using only coins currently in circulation: pennies, nickels, dimes, quarters and half dollars.

This game was popular when I was a boy, but you never see it played today. You can use either an 8x8 or a 10x10 grid. You have as many coins as you need. One player chooses heads, the other tails. Start with four coins in the center cells.

The idea is to make sandwiches. Say you are heads. When you place a coin so that there is heads on each end of a horizontal, vertical, or diagonal line, the coins between the two end ones are turned over. For example, if you place your coin at the end of a line that is TTHTH, it would now become HTTHTH. Now turn over the four center coins and you get HHHTHH. On an 8x8 board, from one to six coins can be sandwiched. On a 10x10 board, from one to eight coins can be sandwiched.

If you can't make a sandwich, you forfeit your turn. But you must play if you can, even if it hurts your score. The game ends when the board is full or neither can play. You win if more than half the coins on the board are heads.

		H	T				
		T	H				

This is a fascinating puzzle. I think it was originated by H. E. Dudeney.

Put four dimes in the top four cells and four pennies in the bottom four cells. You can move as many cells in a diagonal as you please, but at no time can a dime and a penny be on the same diagonal. The trick is to exchange the position of the coins.

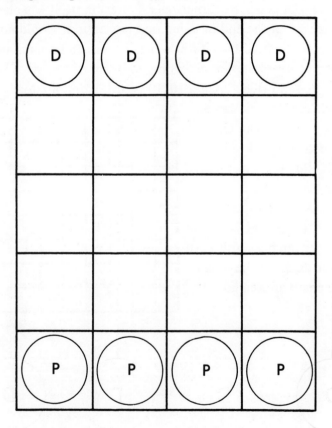

I'm told this game comes from Korea. I don't know, I've never been to Korea. Anyhow, it uses a method of capture unlike that of any other game I know.

You use four dimes and four pennies and start as shown. The players move alternately along the lines, each intersection being a stopping point. You take an opponent's coin by jumping over one of yours and on to his. When not taking a piece, move only one place. The object is to block or to take your opponent's coins.

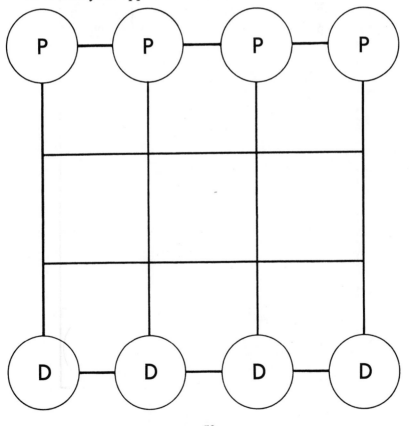

    The card game we call Solitaire is called Patience in Europe. Their Solitaire is played on a board by jumping counters. There is a story that the game was invented by a prisoner in the Bastille. Others say it was imported from the Orient. In any event, I have seen it go through three cycles of popularity in my lifetime.

    A coin is placed in every cell except the center. The object is to jump one coin over another, horizontally or vertically, but not diagonally, and to remove the coin jumped. If you end up with only one coin and that coin in the center cell, you have won the game. Otherwise, try again.

	1	2	3		
	4	5	6		
7	8	9	10	11	12	13
14	15	16	17	18	19	20
21	22	23	24	25	26	27
	28	29	30		
	31	32	33		

Probably everyone has played tic tac toe. It's not much of a game as usually played, but it can be more exciting using coins.

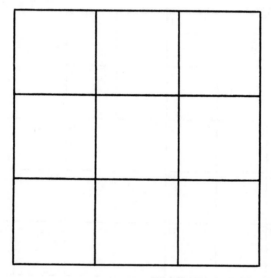

One player has three pennies, the other has three dimes. A tic tac toe diagram is used. The first player places a coin in any cell except the center. Players then alternate until all coins are down. If neither player has won by getting three in a row, each is allowed to move a coin in turn to an adjacent square. However, he can only move horizontally or vertically, not diagonally. The game is won when one player gets three in a row.

The game can also be played on a four by four diagram with each player having four coins.

In France, the game is called *les pendus* (literally, "the hanged") using a five by five diagram and five coins. Diagonal moves are allowed and five similar coins must be aligned to win.

John Scarne invented a game called Teeko. It is played on a 5 by 5 *les pendus* board. Each player has four coins and can move one space in any direction. In addition to getting four in a row, straight or diagonal, the game can be won by assembling them in a square formation in four adjacent cells.

In the Scandinavian countries, a popular variation is The Mill or Nine Men's Morris. It is played on a board of three concentric squares and four transversals. It is, in effect, a triple tic tac toe diagram. One player has nine pennies, the other nine dimes. Each player plays in turn on one of the points (a corner or line intersection) until all eighteen coins have been played. Then each in turn moves one of his coins along any line on which it stands.

Each time a player establishes three coins in a row on any line of the board (called a mill) he is entitled to remove one of his opponent's coins. However, he cannot remove a coin from an opponent's mill. Once a mill is established, the owner can open it by moving one coin off the common line, then close it by moving the coin back.

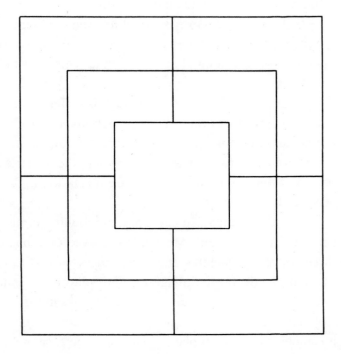

Even though it contains the same coins, a new mill is thus formed and the owner can remove an opponent's coin. When a player is reduced to two coins, the game is over.

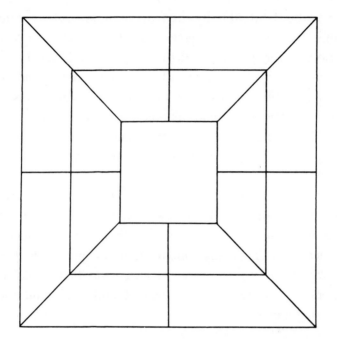

Sometimes, diagonals are added to the diagram, but the play is the same.

Just to show how truly international this type of game is, I will mention the Japanese game of Go Bang or Go Maku. Undoubtedly there are standard rules for this game. However, I've seen several sets of rules. They call, variously, for a 16x16, 18x18, 19x19, or a 20x20 board. Again pennies and dimes can be used for counters and different quantities are used, up to ten of each. The play is the same as in *les pendus* and the object is to get five coins in a row. Some rules allow only vertical and horizontal "fives in a row" to win, others include diagonals.

Still another variation uses no moves. An unlimited number of coins is allowed each player. They are played alternately, again trying to get five in a row, horizontally, vertically, or diagonally. One restriction is put on the play. A player cannot place a coin in such a way that he has two three-in-a-row formations, open at both ends and each utilizing a common coin. For example, in the diagram, he cannot play on squares 7, 9, 18, 21, or 25.

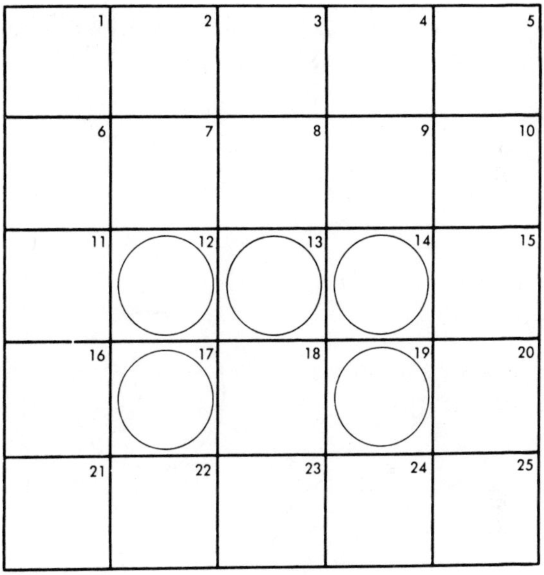
1
2
3
4
5
6
7
8
9
10
11
12
13
14
15
16
17
18
19
20
21
22
23
24
25

Put a penny, a nickel, a dime, a quarter, a half-dollar, and a dollar in a circle in that order. Start with the penny, count clockwise any chosen number and remove that coin. Continue counting and removing coins until only the dollar is left. The trick is what number to choose. Or you can use a penny, four nickels and a dime. Start with the penny and end up with only the dime.

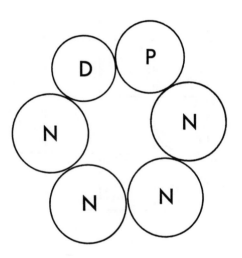

Lay seven coins in a circle, heads up. Starting with any coin, count 1, 2, 3 clockwise and turn the third coin over. Continue doing this, starting with any coin that is heads up and try to turn all the coins over except one. You should have six tails and one head when you finish.

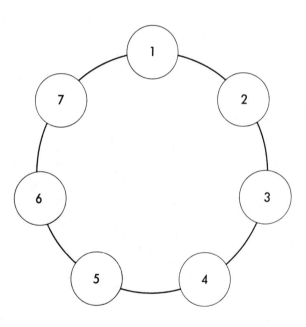

FIVE PENNIES • 55 •

You can put three pennies in a triangle so that all touch each other. You can lay a fourth on top of the three and each of the four touches the other three. Now try arranging five pennies in such a way that each touches the other four.

SHOW ME THE WAY TO GO HOME   • 56 •

Put three pennies on squares 1, 2, and 3 and three dimes on squares 10, 11, and 12. Moving one at a time, pennies and dimes alternately, along the lines from one square to the next, try to exchange places. The catch is that at no time can a penny and a dime be on connected squares (for instance 5 and 12). Only one coin can be in a square at a given time.

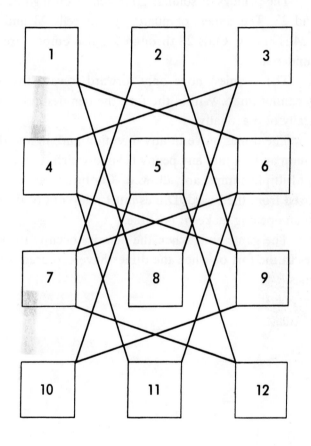

SIEGE

This Dutch game is played with twenty-four pennies and two dimes on the SOLITAIRE diagram.

The pennies or soldiers go in cells 1 through 22 and 26 and 27. The dimes, or guards, go in cells 23 and 25. Cell 24 is empty. Cells 28 through 33, also empty, are the fort under siege.

The pennies move only forward toward the fort. They cannot jump. Within the fort, the pennies move only vertically or diagonally.

The dimes move in any direction and, in addition, can jump and capture any penny beyond which is an empty cell. Multiple jumps are allowed. Captured pennies are removed from the board. Dimes must jump out of the fort when an opening makes it possible.

The game ends when the pennies occupy the nine places in the fort or when the dimes have captured fifteen pennies.

where a is the fewest number of coins that can be drawn, b is the greatest number that can be drawn and n is any number.

In 1907, W. A. Wyhoff complicated the game somewhat. There are two piles of coins. In each draw a player can take any number from one or both piles. But if he elects to draw from both piles, he must take the same number from both. If the loser is the man who takes the last coin, the game is greatly biased in favor of the first player. But if the winner takes the last coin, the game is susceptible to analysis. To win, the safe combinations are 1-2, 3-5, 4-7, 6-10, 8-13, 9-15, 11-18, 12-20, ... The first pair of numbers differ by 1, the second pair by 2, the third by 3, etc.

We now come to the traditional Nim. Here, any number of piles of coins can be used. However, three is the usual number. Players, drawing in turns, can take any number of coins from any one pile, including the entire pile. The loser draws the final coin.

The secret of winning is to present your opponent with a balanced situation. A balanced situation is one in which there is an even number of powers of 2 in each group.

For example, there are 7, 11, and 15 coins in the three piles. They can be pictured thus;

7		4	2	1
11	8		2	1
15	8	4	2	1

There are two 8's and two 4's. In order to balance the group, you take three coins from any pile. As a general rule, when you have such a choice, draw from the greatest pile.

Any play your opponent makes will unbalance the scheme and you simply re-balance it.

The game can be varied by (1) setting a limit on the number of coins that can be drawn at one time, (2) allowing a player to draw a unlimited number of coins from two or more piles (but not all), (3) allowing a player to take a limited number of coins from two or more piles or, (4) if coins are removed from more than one pile, an equal number must be drawn from each pile. Surprisingly, enough, in all these variations, the principle of presenting your opponent with a balanced situation holds.

I have seen the game played by placing 15 or 21 coins in an equilateral triangle.

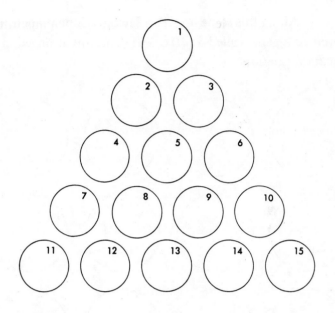

A player can draw any number of touching coins so long as they are in a straight line and on the outside edge of the figure (if coins 1, 2, and 3 have been drawn, 4, 5, and 6 will be outside coins). I've never seen a description of this game in print so I guess it has never been analyzed. And I haven't played it enough to advise you on proper strategy.

Along this same line, Piet Hein of Copenhagen has invented a game called TacTix. The coins are arranged in a square formation.

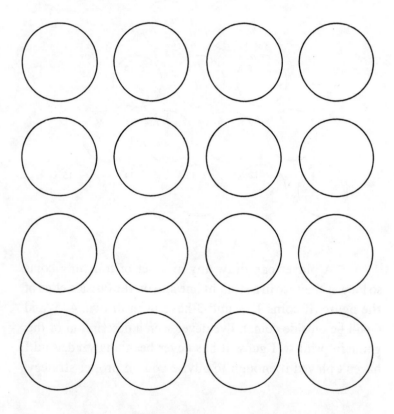

Players alternately remove coins from any horizontal or vertical row. They must always be adjoining coins with no gaps between them. The player drawing the last coin loses. The 4x4 game has been analyzed, but again, no winning strategy has been devised.

A certain prison has nine cells which are connected as shown.

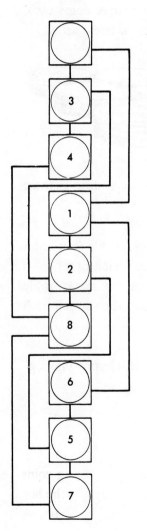

Pennies represent the eight prisoners. In as few moves as possible, move the prisoners so they line up 1, 2, 3, 4, 5, 6, 7, 8. No two prisoners can be in a cell at the same time and at least seven prisoners must be in cells at all times.

I'll close this brouhaha with my own invention. I call it Cube-O. It is really a combination of the last two games. You start out with nine stacks of three coins each, or with sixteen stacks of four coins each in cubic array.

Players alternate in removing the coins according to these rules.

1. The top coin of any stack
2. Any two coins in a row, stack, or file (but not a diagonal) provided they touch each other
3. Any three (or four) coins in a row stack, or file (but not a diagonal) provided they touch each other
4. The player who removes the last coin loses.

Again, I cannot advise you on strategy. But happy playing!

• 1 •

SOLUTIONS

Leave 13 blank.

1.	4 to 13	5.	13 to 6	9.	6 to 1
2.	3 to 8	6.	7 to 2	10.	1 to 4
3.	1 to 4	7.	11 to 13	11.	4 to 13
4.	10 to 3	8.	14 to 12	12.	12 to 14
				13.	15 to 13

• 2 •

Leave 6 blank.

1.	4 to 6	5.	6 to 4	9.	14 to 12
2.	11 to 4	6.	7 to 2	10.	12 to 5
3.	12 to 5	7.	1 to 4	11.	4 to 6
4.	2 to 7	8.	10 to 8	12.	3 to 10
				13.	15 to 6

• 3 •

1.	13 to 11	5.	3 to 10	9.	6 to 4
2.	4 to 13	6.	15 to 6	10.	7 to 2
3.	11 to 4	7.	14 to 12	11.	1 to 4
4.	10 to 8	8.	2 to 7	12.	4 to 13
				13.	13 to 11

• 4 •

Shift 7 to the left of 2, 10 to the right of 3, and 1 below and between 8 and 9.

• 5 •

1. p1 p2 p3 · n3 n2 n1
2. p1 p2 · p3 n3 n2 n1
3. p1 p2 n3 p3 · n2 n1
4. p1 p2 n3 p3 n2 · n1
5. p1 p2 n3 · n2 p3 n1
6. p1 · n3 p2 n2 p3 n1
7. · p1 n3 p2 n2 p3 n1
8. n3 p1 · p2 n2 p3 n1

9. n3 p1 n2 p2 · p3 n1
10. n3 p1 n2 p2 n1 p3 ·
11. n3 p1 n2 p2 n1 · p3
12. n3 p1 n2 · n1 p2 p1
13. n3 · n2 p1 n1 p2 p3
14. n3 n2 · p1 n1 p2 p3
15. n3 n2 n1 p1 · p2 p3
16. n3 n2 n1 · p1 p2 p3

1. p1 p2 p3 p4 · n4 n3 n2 n1
2. p1 p2 p3 · p4 n4 n3 n2 n1
3. p1 p2 p3 n4 p4 · n3 n2 n1
4. p1 p2 p3 n4 p4 n3 · n2 n1
5. p1 p2 p3 n4 · n3 p4 n2 n1
6. p1 p2 · n4 p3 n3 p4 n2 n1
7. p1 · p2 n4 p3 n3 p4 n2 n1
8. p1 n4 p2 · p3 n3 p4 n2 n1
9. p1 n4 p2 n3 p3 · p4 n2 n1
10. p1 n4 p2 n3 p3 n2 p4 · n1
11. p1 n4 p2 n3 p3 n2 p4 n1 ·
12. p1 n4 p2 n3 p3 n2 · n1 p4
13. p1 n4 p2 n3 · n2 p3 n1 p4

14. p1 n4 · n3 p2 n2 p3 n1 p4
15. · n4 p1 n3 p2 n2 p3 n1 p4
16. n4 · n3 p1 p2 n2 p3 n1 p4
17. n4 n3 p1 · p2 n2 p3 n1 p4
18. n4 n3 p1 n2 p2 · p3 n1 p4
19. n4 n3 p1 n2 p2 n1 p3 · p4
20. n4 n3 p1 n2 p2 n1 · p3 p4
21. n4 n3 p1 n2 · n1 p2 p3 p4
22. n4 n3 · n2 p1 n1 p2 p3 p4
23. n4 n3 n2 · p1 n1 p2 p3 p4
24. n4 n3 n2 n1 p1 · p2 p3 p4
25. n4 n3 n2 n1 · p1 p2 p3 p4

• 6 •

1. N-8 to cell 9
2. P-8 to cell 10
3. P-7 to cell 8
4. N-8 to cell 7
5. N-6 to cell 9
6. P-6 to cell 12
7. P-3 to cell 6
8. N-6 to cell 3
9. N-3 to cell 9
10. N-2 to cell 15
11. P-8 to cell 16
12. P-7 to cell 10
13. N-3 to cell 8
14. N-7 to cell 9
15. N-4 to cell 11
16. P-6 to cell 14
17. P-3 to cell 12
18. P-5 to cell 6

19.	N-3 to cell 5	29.	P-3 to cell 13	39.	N-2 to cell 9
20.	P-2 to cell 8	30.	P-5 to cell 12	40.	P-5 to cell 15
21.	P-1 to cell 2	31.	P-4 to cell 6	41.	P-4 to cell 12
22.	N-8 to cell 1	32.	N-7 to cell 4	42.	N-2 to cell 6
23.	N-7 to cell 7	33.	N-4 to cell 7	43.	N-1 to cell 9
24.	N-4 to cell 9	34.	N-5 to cell 9	44.	P-4 to cell 11
25.	N-1 to cell 11	35.	P-2 to cell 10	45.	P-1 to cell 10
26.	P-8 to cell 17	36.	P-1 to cell 8	46.	N-1 to cell 8
27.	P-7 to cell 16	37.	N-6 to cell 2		
28.	N-5 to cell 10	38.	N-5 to cell 3		

• 7 •

Move 1 around as indicated by the arrow; then carefully slide coin 4 out of its place and up to the position left open by coin 1.

• 8 •

Move coin 1 to dotted position 1. Move coin 2 to dotted position 2. Slide coin 4 into place originally occupied by coin 2. Move coin 1 back to its original place.

Move A to touch B and D

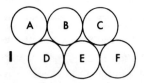

Move D to touch E and F

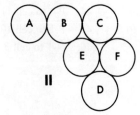

Move A to touch D and E

Move E to touch A and B below

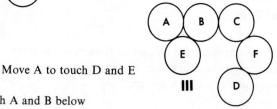

10

The trick is to leave your opponent an even number of similar groups, such as 0.0.000.000. Whatever he does in one group, you repeat in a similar group. If he draws a single, you draw the other single. If he draws two from a triplet, you draw two from the other triplet. If he draws the center one from a triplet, you draw the center one from the other triplet.

The first player can always win by taking either the fourth or eighth kayle from the right leaving either 0.000.0000000 or 0.0000000.000. Whatever the second player does, the first can then resolve the pattern into the even numbers of similar groups.

• 13 •

Turn over pairs 3-4, 4-5, and 2-3

• 14 •

	STRAIGHT	REVERSE
Start	x x N P N P N *P N* P	x x N P N P N *P N* P
After first move	P N N P *N P* N x x P	N P N *P N* P N x x P
After second move	P *N N* P x x N N P P	N *P N* x x P N N P P
After third move	P x x P N N N N *P P*	N x x N P P *N N* P P
After fourth move	P P P P N N N N x x	N N N N P P P P x x

• 15 •

1. Put 7 on 10	*or*	1. Put 4 on 1
2. Put 5 on 2		2. Put 6 on 9
3. Put 3 on 8		3. Put 8 on 3
4. Put 1 on 4		4. Put 10 on 7
5. Put 9 on 6		5. Put 2 on 5

Considering a stack of two coins as one.

1. Put 7 on 10	*or*	1. Put 4 on 1
2. Put 5 on 2		2. Put 3 on 8
3. Put 3 on 8		3. Put 1 on 6
4. Put 1 on 6		4. Put 10 on 5
5. Put 9 on 4		5. Put 2 on 7

79

• 16 •

	a	b	c	d	e	f
A.	1	0	4	6	0	3
B.	1	3	6	0	0	2
C.	1	4	0	5	0	2
D.	1	4	0	5	2	0
E.	1	6	0	0	2	5
F.	1	6	0	3	0	4
G.	2	0	1	4	0	5
H.	2	0	1	6	0	5
I.	2	0	5	1	0	4

	a	b	c	d	e	f
J.	2	0	6	1	0	4
K.	2	4	1	0	0	5
L.	2	5	0	0	1	4
M.	2	5	0	6	3	0
N.	2	6	0	0	1	5
O.	2	6	1	0	0	5
P.	2	6	1	0	4	0
Q.	3	0	6	1	0	4

If reversals and reflections are allowed, there are 120 ways to solve the puzzle.

• 17 •

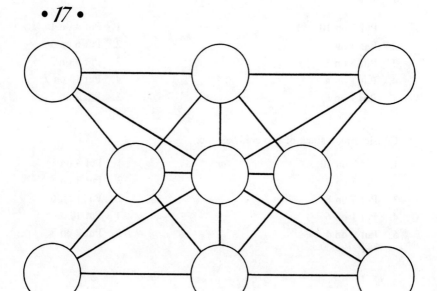

• 18 •

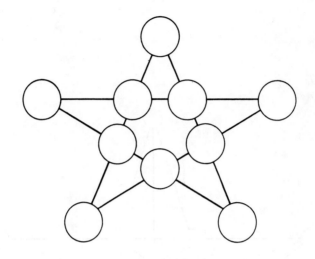

• 19 •

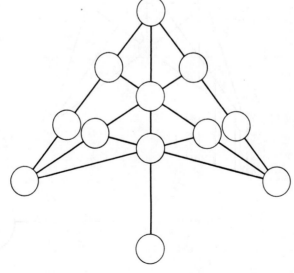

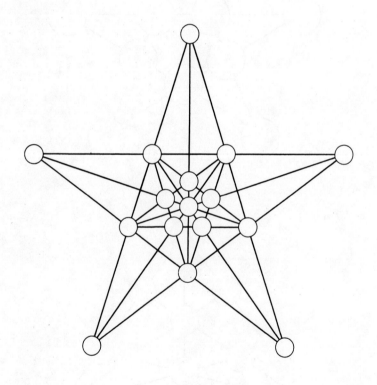

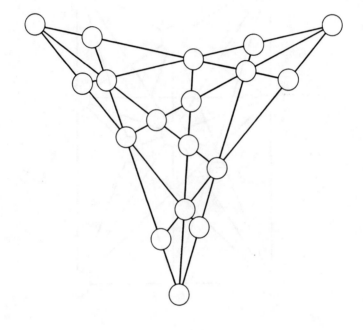

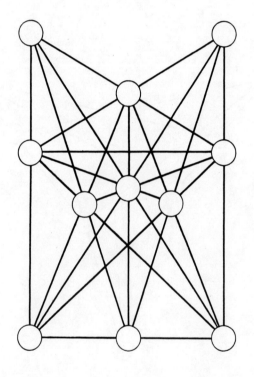

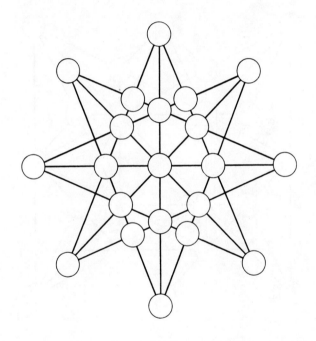

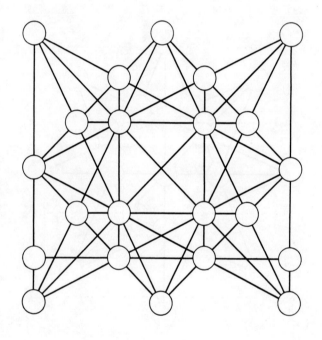

• 25 •

Twelve is the greatest number

• 26 •

1. Move 5 over 8, 9, 3, 1.
2. Move 7 over 4.
3. Move 6 over 2 and 7.
4. Move 5 over 6.

• 27 •

Transfer a coin from square 8 to square 10, then play as follows, always removing the coin jumped over.

1. 9 to 11
2. 1 to 9
3. 13 to 5
4. 16 to 8
5. 4 to 12
6. 12 to 10
7. 3 to 1
8. 1 to 9
9. 9 to 11

• 28 •

15 CENTS

1. 7 on 3
2. 5 on 10
3. 9 on 7
4. 12 on 8
5. 4 on 5
6. 11 on 12
7. 2 on 6
8. 1 on 2

20 CENTS

1. 8 on 3
2. 9 on 14
3. 1 on 5
4. 16 on 12
5. 7 on 8
6. 10 on 7
7. 6 on 9
8. 15 on 16
9. 13 on 1
10. 4 on 15
11. 2 on 13
12. 11 on 6

• 29 •

1-N, 2-P, 3-N, 4-N, 5-P, 6-N, 7-P, 8-P.

• 30 •

1. 1 to 5
2. 3 to 7 to 1
3. 8 to 4 to 3 to 7
4. 6 to 2 to 8 to 4 to 3
5. 5 to 6 to 2 to 8
6. 1 to 5 to 6
7. 7 to 1

• *32* •

1. 2 to 1	4. 6 to 3	7. 1 to 4	10. 7 to 6
2. 5 to 2	5. 7 to 6	8. 3 to 1	
3. 3 to 5	6. 4 to 7	9. 6 to 3	

• *33* •

1. 5 to 8, remove 7	4. 10 to 6, remove 8	7. 5 to 8, remove 7
2. 2 to 5, remove 4	5. 1 to 4, remove 2	8. 6 to 10, remove 8
3. 9 to 2, remove 6	6. 3 to 7, remove 4	

• *34* •

1. 1 right	9. 1 on 4	17. 1 center	25. 1 on 4
2. 2 left	10. 2 center	18. 2 on 5	26. 2 left
3. 1 on 2	11. 1 on 2	19. 1 on 2	27. 1 on 2
4. 3 right	12. 3 on 4	20. 3 center	28. 3 on 4
5. 1 center	13. 1 right	21. 1 on 4	29. 1 center
6. 2 on 3	14. 2 on 3	22. 2 on 3	30. 2 on 3
7. 1 on 2	15. 1 on 2	23. 1 on 2	31. 1 on 2
8. 4 left	16. 5 right	24. 4 on 5	

• *35* •

1. 1 to 10	9. 27 to 18	17. 32 to 18
2. 7 to 14	10. 5 to 23	18. 25 to 15
3. 17 to 10	11. 26 to 19	19. 29 to 11
4. 21 to 7	12. 16 to 23	20. 20 to 7
5. 2 to 11	13. 12 to 26	21. 3 to 10
6. 8 to 15	14. 31 to 22	22. 24 to 6
7. 4 to 18	15. 13 to 26	23. 28 to 1
8. 9 to 23	16. 30 to 23	

• 36 •

Place the extra man on square 7

1. 2 to 11	6. 5 to 23	11. 32 to 18
2. 20 to 7	7. 12 to 26	12. 29 to 15
3. 3 to 10	8. 31 to 22	13. 28 to 10
4. 1 to 15	9. 13 to 26	14. 21 to 7
5. 4 to 18	10. 30 to 23	

• 37 •

Move the counters four times in the following sequence: 2, 4, 6, 8, 7, 5, 3, 1. Next move the counters 2, 4, 6, 8 and the reversal is complete.

• 39 •

1. 2 to 3	7. 8 to 6	13. 5 to 3
2. 9 to 4	8. 5 to 10	14. 10 to 8
3. 10 to 7	9. 6 to 9	15. 4 to 7
4. 3 to 8	10. 2 to 5	16. 3 to 2
5. 4 to 2	11. 1 to 6	17. 8 to 1
6. 7 to 5	12. 6 to 4	18. 7 to 10

• 40 •

(a-bc) indicates coin a is moved to touch b and c.
(1-56), (3-14), (4-58), (5-23), (2-54)
(D-CE), (G-CD), (D-CG), (G-BD), (C-AG), (A-BE), (E-FH).

• 41 •

Weighing 1: either one coin in the group 1, 2, 3, 4 is heavy or one coin in the group 5, 6, 7, 8 is light. 9, 10, 11, 12 are normal.

Weighing 2: Either coin 3 or 4 is heavy or 5 is light because 9, 10, 11 are normal and 6 and 7 come from the light side of weighing 1.

Weighing 3: Coins 3 and 4 balance, hence 5 is the counterfeit and is light.

• *43* •

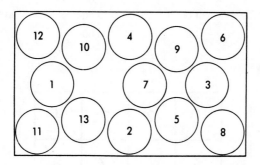

• *44* •

H	N	Q	P	D
Q	P	D	H	N
D	H	N	Q	P
N	Q	P	D	H
P	D	H	N	Q

Q H	H N	P Q	N P	D D
N Q	D P	Q D	H H	P N
H D	P H	N N	D Q	Q P
D N	Q Q	H P	P D	N H
P P	N D	D H	Q N	H Q

• *47* •

292

If you are interested in other amounts, here they are;

Amount	Number of ways to make change	Amount	Number of ways to make change
.25	13	2.00	2728
.50	50	3.00	12611
.75	134	4.00	41564
1.00	292	5.00	115022

• *49* •

1	2	3	4
5	6	7	8
9	10	11	12
13	14	15	16
17	18	19	20

Using the above notation, play as follows;

PENNIES	DIMES	PENNIES	DIMES
1. 18-15	1. 3-6	4. 15-5	4. 6-16
2. 17-8	2. 4-13	5. 8-3	5. 13-18
3. 19-14	3. 2-7	6. 14-9	6. 7-12

PENNIES	DIMES	PENNIES	DIMES
7. 5-10	7. 16-11	13. 19-16	13. 2-5
8. 9-19	8. 12-2	14. 16-1	14. 5-20
9. 10-4	9. 11-17	15. 9-6	15. 12-15
10. 20-10	10. 1-11	16. 13-7	16. 8-14
11. 3-9	11. 18-12	17. 6-3	17. 15-18
12. 10-13	12. 11-8	18. 7-2	18. 14-19

• 51 •

Here is one of many solutions;

29-17, 26-24, 17-29, 33-25, 32-24, 24-26, 27-25, 13-27, 12-26, 18-30, 27-25, 30-18, 22-24, 31-23, 24-22, 21-23, 7-21, 8-22, 16-28, 21-23, 28-16, 10-12, 3-11, 18-6, 1-3, 3-11, 12-10, 5-17, 17-15, 4-16, 15-17.

• 53 •

27 or 29

• 54 •

Always start with the coin that is two back of the coin you started with previously. In other words, the coin you start with on this move is the coin turned over on the next page.

a. Start with 1, turn over 3
b. Start with 6, turn over 1
c. Start with 4, turn over 6

d. Start with 2, turn over 4
e. Start with 7, turn over 2
f. Start with 5, turn over 7

• 55 •

Place coins 1 and 2 on top of 3 as shown; stand 4 and 5 on edge across exposed parts of 3 and hold them together so that they touch each other.

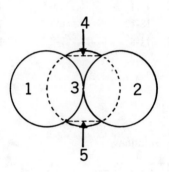

• 56 •

	DIME	PENNY		DIME	PENNY
1.	10-5	1-8	7.	12-7	3-4
2.	11-6	2-9	8.	1-8	10-5
3.	12-7	3-4	9.	6-1	9-10
4.	5-12	8-3	10.	7-2	4-11
5.	6-1	9-10	11.	8-3	5-12
6.	7-6	4-9			

• 59 •

Move the prisoners in this order:

1, 2, 3, 1, 2, 6, 5, 3, 1, 2, 6, 5, 3, 1, 2, 4, 8, 7, 1, 2, 4, 8, 7, 4, 5, 6.